An anthology of
writing and art by women in mid-life

Compiled and produced by
Mary Manandhar, Maureen Howley and Ita Conroy

with additional photography by Peter Wilcock

Sold in aid of the Sligo Cancer Support Centre

MID-LIFE SLICES: An anthology of writing and art by women in mid-life

Complied and produced by Mary Manandhar, Maureen Howley and Ita Conroy

With additional photography by Peter Wilcock

Sold in aid of the Sligo Cancer Support Centre

Graphic Design by Jackie McMullen, Sapphire Design, Maugherow, Co. Sligo, Ireland   www.sapphiredesign.ie

Published by Molly's Press, County Clare, Ireland

Printed in Ireland by KPS Colour Print Ltd, Knock, Co. Mayo, Ireland   www.kpscolourprint.com

www.mid-lifeslices.com

www.facebook.com/midlifeslicesbookproject

ISBN 978-0-9567039-1-0

RRP €12

The members of the Mid-Life Slices Team acknowledge and thank

For book design and production

- Carol McNamara of Molly's Press, Co. Clare, for encouragement and publishing expertise
- Peter Wilcock, for the distinctive logo, his additional original photographs and photos of the art submissions
- Jackie McMullen/Dickon Whitehead of Sapphire Design & DW Photography, for graphic design and photo-editing
- Brendan Salmon of KPS Colour Print, Knock, for printing and production
- Beatrice Murray and Adriana Gradea, for proof reading
- Paula Lahiff, for all her contributions in the early stages of the project

For the book launch on Saturday 28th April 2012

- Marian Harkin MEP, for her endorsement and the launch of the book
- Ray and Eileen Monahan, for their generous sponsorship of the launch
- Niamh Crowley and some of the cast of the Fun Company's 'All Shook Up', for entertainment
- The Model, Sligo, particularly Tara McGowan

For the fundraising gig on 26th November 2011, and other promotional support

- The Harp Tavern on Quay Street, Sligo, particularly Sean Dwyer
- 'Cosmic Banditos' band members: Anna Leddy, Ide Leddy, Maire O'Gara, David Pierce, Mary Roche
- 'Let's Have Six' band members: Brian Cawley, Paul Howley, Terry McGlynn, Paddy Monahan, Sally O'Connor, Jack Pope
- All the local businesses who gave prizes for the night
- Eamonn McManus of TigerPrint, Sligo, for promotional materials
- Jack Conroy, Mark Howley and Ashok Manandhar for youthful vigour and help

For being the reason why this book exists

- Maureen Durcan and the staff at the Sligo Cancer Support Centre, for inspiration
- All our women contributors who allowed us glimpses of their slices of mid-life

Foreword

As you meander through the pages of this book you will find that the ordinary becomes extraordinary and the everyday is viewed through an imaginative lens that reminds us of the wonder of life and living.

There is a real sense of hope in the many contributions, partnered by the tightly woven bonds of friendship and the continuity of love. The vulnerability that we feel at times, the fragility of life – it's all here, but so too is the joy, the celebration, the compassion, the understanding, the self-acceptance and the determination to wring every last drop out of life. As one contributor puts it, "mid life slices, never better, never more bold".

The fear that love may fade or die and then the huge surge of relief when we realise that despite all, in one way or another, love endures; that realisation casts a warm glow. So does the sense that it is within your power to be one of the lucky few as you ask the question, can I accept the invitations of life? Looking into the mirror who do you see, can you reach out to life and pull it close?

I still wonder – how to cherish the ladies. I gained insights on being Grandma and on not being Grandma. I smiled, I grinned, I laughed out loud. I felt a bond, a kind of womanly closeness. I nodded in a kind of feminine comprehension. I envied the one who can still hit high C and I admired the lady who played the hand she was dealt with wry humour and assistance from her chiropractor. I was briefly stopped in my tracks by the woman who had perfect timing, and I clapped out loud in pure celebration for the woman who still says "I do, I do, I do".

Our fragilities are exposed, a coward in the dark. Our vulnerabilities become visible. Stories of love lost, or a death foretold, of searing loss simply spoken, of human frailty and human foibles, await you. There is a raging against the dimming of the light, yet a quiet acceptance of life moving on. It is comforting to know that, as one grows older, it's great to have the freedom without needing to explain, but equally we don't escape reflections on the barrenness of death. Touching memories of how the islands of the mind grow small: that piece reminded me of a line from a song called 'The Dutchman' hauntingly sung by the late Liam Clancy which simply says "Long ago I used to be a young man, and dear Margaret remembers that for me."

We stumble upon chance meetings, we discover blended families and there are menopausal moments to be celebrated. The ordinary, the flu, the worn jumper, the battle of the middle age spread sits comfortably alongside the extraordinary, the streak of pleasure keenly felt, the determination to let no day pass without an event and dreaming of swims on Bertra beach.

We are invited to take faltering steps in a dance of discovery, to grasp small blessings and the possibilities of now, and to delight in living with its purpose and promise. On being 50, on reaching 60, 'will you still need me, will you still feed me,' Country music, three chords and the truth, lives unfold, stories told. Unexpected emotion catches you: The News of the World, 'in memory of my father'. So too will the jolt of the unexpected as it rips your heart and punches you in the stomach.

A stitch in time, the march of time as it legs it, remind us to take time.

Take time to read this collection, to feel the warmth of its touch, to be inspired by its creativity and to feel the sheer delight of life and its possibilities, and then - the real trick - use your time.

Independent Member of the European Parliament

Ireland North and West Constituency

www.marianharkin.com

Introduction

In spring 2011, a mid-life milestone brought us all together, a 50th birthday occasion with Cava bubbling in tall glasses, some cheese, crackers and probably chocolate. There was talk of making it to the half-century, and then talk of those who hadn't made it that far and a suggestion that we remember them while also celebrating this time in our lives. It all sounded grand then, but perhaps not the best laid planning for a major project! So sure, it's been a challenge, but we got here in the end.

We put out a call for submissions wondering if anyone would respond. But in they came, a diverse collection of 87 individual voices and imagery from women in, or connected to, Sligo, Leitrim, West Cavan. Some pieces are from seasoned, even published, writers, while others are from those very new to writing. Art comes from well-known artists who exhibit in our public spaces, as well as from those who show only in the privacy of their own corner. What all these people have in common is a willingness to share their innermost thoughts and feelings, in words or art, and so support the Sligo Cancer Support Centre. We feel honoured to have been entrusted with them, and by people we have mostly never met. We kept our editing touch very light to keep as close as possible to the essence of the writer's own voice.

As the anthology took shape, our four themes emerged to unite us in a celebration of how we change, feel, love and remember. Through our writing and drawing and sewing and painting and pointing our cameras, we speak out, express ourselves and raise our mid-life voices. Here we are!

Mary, Maureen and Ita   Sligo, April 2012

This book is dedicated to all our women friends and family members, past and present, who have completed, or are still on, their journey of battling cancer. We celebrate your lives in this anthology.

A Changing slice of mid-life

A Feeling slice of mid-life

A Loving slice of mid-life

A Remembering slice of mid-life

A Changing slice of mid-life

"The only constant is change."   *Heroclitus of Ephesus*

In this first section of 'Mid-Life Slices', women acknowledge their changing views of self. They speak of how physical forms, with all their vulnerabilities and alterations, belie what is going on in their heads. The younger self is still very much alive, with images caught and suspended in an earlier frame. In different creative modes, these women reflect on how their relationships change with loss of partners and identities; but they also celebrate new emerging chapters in life and love. Some talk of discovering new freedoms and the casting aside of pre-conceived notions that are held by society, and sometimes family and friends. They acknowledge simple pleasures and evaluate what matters as mid-life throws up challenges and opportunities for personal growth. Some find a new appreciation of abundance.

Throughout the work seeps a sense of knowing that change is inevitable. Whether we face an empty nest, separation, loss, or a period of transition, we have a choice in how we deal with the hand of life. It is so encouraging that, as women, we can bear witness to these winds of change with so much creative energy and vitality. There is undoubtedly freedom to celebrate now, care less about how others view us and be more true to who we really are. It is where we have been that gave us these unique and many coloured experiences that continue to define us into, and beyond, mid-life.

Ita

Sleeping arrangements

Through twenty seven married years
she slept on the left
curled on her side
facing out
he slept on the right
curled around her
warm breath on her neck
drifting to blissed oblivion.

Bed was mecca, hub, haven
where hurts healed
minds emptied, refilled
bodies caressed, rested
babies began, nested, fed
worries emerged, dispersed
fragile spirits steadied.

For four years after he died
she still slept on the left
curled on her side
facing out
imagining him
curled around her

warm breath on her neck
and sometimes facing in
towards the empty space.

Then one night she uncurled
lay on her back
right leg bent at the knee
arms loose at her sides
and the next night and so on
then she took away
his two pillows
headprint-less for years
and began to centre
herself in the bed.

Soon she would be ready
to leave it completely
and make new arrangements
taking with her only the memory
of his warm breath
on her neck.

Kathy Pearse

Transition: transmission **Kim Doherty**

Dance of discovery: discovery of dance

Twisting and swirling

spinning

floating

the dance is inside, coming out.

And each appears and play their part,

the toddler, little girl,

teenager, young woman,

and all meld beautifully into the woman that is. Now.

Divided by two

is closer the mark

to what clock and calendar

might say.

And each spin, each twirl rewinds the clock,

and a night of dancing tears a full page from the calendar.

Bríd Brady

Advantages

There are distinct advantages to arriving at the middle years. But before turning to them, in case you think I have lost my marbles, I want to lay my cards on the table. That is if I can find them! To be honest, I was never tip-top in the finding things department, but have gradually arrived in the land of "'Anyone seen my keys? Where did I leave my friggin' glasses?" And somewhat worryingly, "'Jaysus, I could have sworn I parked the car there!'"

Cards on the table also reminds me to tell you that, although only in my 50s, I am struggling a bit with pains in both my thumbs. That's despite faithful administration of a really awfully painful exercise learned from a physiotherapist friend, which apparently stops the stringy bits on the inside sticking to your joints. She explained it better than that at the time and, while I am fairly sure I am doing it right, there is not much relief. I am acutely aware of my thumbs now and I used not to notice them much. I can see them clearly, which is more than I can say for the cards across the table. Alternating between corrective glasses and things I can no longer see with them, like numbers on cards, is really a bloody nuisance.

As long as I have clothes and shoes on, I am ready for out. Bob's your uncle – and he won't notice me anyway because I am almost invisible. I do get the occasional sympathetic 'we are in this together' glance from the greys. I used to get seen. Probably hit my peak at about 16 – quite a while ago – but I have fond memories. I also have a theory. Half-baked as it may be, here's how it goes: our species' survival requires us to be primed to notice, interact with, and ultimately get on with our peers to maximise our chances of procreation. A key ingredient in this unconscious [how kind am I?] signalling is the female waist-hip ratio. And there's the rub. I could be described as being in reasonable condition but the curve in the middle has definitely filled out. I even find myself attracted to the 'comfortable waist' section of the Marks and Spencer jeans racks. A possible upside is that there is no need now for younger womenfolk to carry out that lightning quick assessment of my status as possible competitor.

Did I say there were distinct advantages? Ah yes. My skin has mysteriously thickened. For instance, I don't let the fact that I have only the most fragile of grasps on how to play the bass guitar get in the way of occasional performances with a bunch of forgiving friends in our alternative country music band. Actually I am free to make of myself what I will, in the sure knowledge that no one will notice, much less care. No need to wear all that bloody purple unless the mood takes me. I know I can have friends of all ages – it just requires the more solid base of a relationship acquired through reaching out and having meaningful conversation. I may even be reaching emotional maturity.

I bet the day will come when the neuroscientists will discover a hitherto unrealised spurt of brain development through to, and beyond, middle age, which will explain all this executive functioning. Until then, I find myself wondering how well I would get on with so and so if we were parked beside each other on rocking chairs in an old folk's home. Would they tell a good story, for example? Sure, isn't that what it's all about in the end?

Mary Roche

I am

I am sliced by
time watching
shadows
creep closer
tickling the
only spot
I've kept
hidden
the last
corner in
headlights.

Patricia Curran-Mulligan

DNA

I am
somebody
new each
time
I pass a
looking
glass,
today I
see my
mother.

Patricia Curran-Mulligan

Don't call me Grandma

Let's get one thing straight. I am not a Granny. I don't have any grandchildren bouncing on my knee or sending me homemade cards with glitter star stickers at Christmas. I'm no-one's Nan. Most definitely, nobody calls me Grandma.

But the other day, when I was minding a friend's toddler in a hotel garden as the friend had gone inside to order drinks, an elderly couple complimented me on my 'adorable grandchild'.

"He's very cute," they continued in their innocence, while I was suddenly finding it hard to breathe. "How old is he? Twelve months? Lovely eyes." They smiled down at the boy in the stroller and cooed in his face.

Of course, at fifty-one, I could easily be a grandparent. I could have a son or daughter in their twenties (*let's face it, even in their thirties*), and their offspring would be my grandchildren. Perfectly feasible. Not at all unusual. And not a bother for many people. I know that fifty is 'the new thirty', and sixty is 'the new forty' (*I can't wait*), and that, out there, plenty of yummy grannies defy the ageing process. Probably millions of fifty-one-year-olds are proud to show off their grandchildren to anyone who will listen, but not me.

In my own perception of myself, mistaking me for a granny is the equivalent of giving me a bus pass. Or handing me a pair of comfy slippers and registering me into a retirement home on the south coast to spend my days watching passers by from an armchair, and my evenings with knitting and bingo.

Not that there's anything wrong with that. It's just not me. I still have too much to do, experiences to be had (*within reason*), rivers to cross (*with stout stick*), mountains to climb (*slowly and with knee supports*), love affairs to hope for (*with the lights off*). Don't I?

In my head, I am a lithe and active twenty-something with the long mane of the auburn hair I was born with, unlined skin, sex appeal and a taste for the adventurous life. Speaking from my not-quite-in-the-realms-of-reality mindset, I don't have aching joints or saggy breasts or double chin(s) or middle-aged spread or a pelvic floor that needs lifting. I don't wear bifocal glasses and orthopaedic footwear or have trouble reading miniscule labels on food packaging and tiny texts on mobile phone displays. When I catch myself in the mirror (*very rarely from choice*) or see myself in a photo (*even more rarely if I have anything to do with it*), I experience private awkward moments much like the granny-labelling incident. But these are only fleeting glances, quickly pushed aside and buried, along with that head of mine, into the proverbial sand. I have a highly developed ability (*some may say delusion*) to revert to another earlier vision of me. That's the real me, right?

OK, maybe not. But last time I checked my CV, graduating to Grandmother status was not listed as one of my achievements or key competencies. No, I'm not yet ready for that. Not one bit. So don't call me Grandma.

Mary Manandhar

Blended families

We met later in life you and I.

There were mine and yours,

five in all and five grandchildren,

not one living here anymore,

Australia, Galway, London.

Our personal diaspora,

at times rushing through,

sometimes fused, sometimes alone,

a heritage of children.

Lately a scatter of newly-bought wellingtons

and a plaque on the wall

'Gran and Grandad – memories are made here'

are all that remain of a clannish gathering.

A heady cocktail, swooping through,

all with their different pasts and life stories.

This blend is sometimes powerful, sometimes fragile

with unspoken experiences and lack of common history

save you and I.

And yet on autumn days filled with nostalgia

our unique family, although diverse, seems possible,

as I sit and reflect in our home of photographs.

Ita Conroy

Mother and daughter   Maria Bagnoli

Changing my number

I laughed when I was asked to take part in this wonderful project to celebrate women in mid-life. My questioning reply was "Who? Me? What would I write about? I wouldn't have a clue!" Maureen kindly advised me to write something from a positive angle. So, I eventually put pen to paper.

I recall some years ago, on the eve of my fortieth birthday, confiding in my family that I was dreading the thought of reaching that particular milestone. One of our darling young daughters wisely remarked "What are you worried about, mum? You are only changing your number!"

I have come to realise the wisdom of that youthful comment. I realise how lucky I am to have reached mid-life intact, with the gift of good health, both physically and mentally. To be able to get up each day and try to do my very best, honestly and with integrity, is indeed a gift.

To see the reflection of my husband and myself in the beautiful faces of our children is a gift.

To have the hindsight of years of experience is a gift.

To hear the wind howl on a stormy night and have the vision to see that the storm will pass is also a gift.

In these harsh economic times of constant and relentless discussion, we must focus on the positives. I celebrate and enjoy the simple things of life:

To be able to bake and smell a home-baked cake is charming

To walk for miles – come rain or shine

To be able to laugh, love and still enjoy the company of my husband,

from youth to mid-life

To be able to sing and reach 'high C'

To have a roof over my head

To have wonderful family and friends

To have a job and a career

To have faith

To laugh out loud

To talk to yourself

To have the wisdom of years

To have 'crow's feet'

To be happy to continue, and enjoy

.... changing my number.

Ann Hayes

Flying the nest

The time has come for you to leave
and fly like a dandelion in the breeze,
content to soar and scatter over random soil
arriving where your destiny decrees.
But just before you go your separate way,
consider who you are today,
for already you have paved a path and left a mark
indelible as love-struck letters carved in bark.

You have learned respect for self and others:
those whose words of wisdom guide
and those who have no voice, but still have pride
when prejudice has nowhere left to hide.
You have known the strength of family and friendship
built with solid bricks that time defies,
and laughed at nothing more than laughter
and the joy that memories evoke long after laughter dies.

And you will leave the footprint of your spirit
as you spread your wings to fly,
with roots that cannot be destroyed
by passing storms or long goodbyes.
You will rise to heights not yet imagined
and sometimes sink with ego bruised and sore,
then you will close your eyes and let the years rewind
to when your dreams and schemes flew through this open door.

So if you ever doubt yourself and life
remember who you are today.
If temptation beckons with a twisted finger
remember who you are today.
And if despair sits close and whispers in your ear
remember who you are today.
And no matter where you are or what you do
remember that we're always here for you.

Maureen Howley

Never more than a call away   Laura Bell

Naked

Here I stand,
naked,
on the page.

Not naked as the day I was born,
all needy
and innocent.

Not naked as in the first blush of youth,
modest,
but full of promise.

But naked,
exposed,
vulnerable,
as never before.
Stretch marks and sagging breasts
displayed
for all the world to see.

Not naked and unashamed.
But naked,
frightened,
alone,
and ready to begin.

Pippa Black

Middle-age spread

I swing my two feet out of the bed on to the floor to ground myself.

I am OK this morning, I say, mentally checking myself all over. *I know my name – well, that's a positive.* This is closely followed by my mantra: *I am not going to eat fattening foods today.*

I move across the floor to the bathroom, stepping through my imaginary door into my sacred space – which happens to be the shower this morning.

You're starving, aren't you? That little voice whispers in my ear.

No, I am not, I spit back. *I am eating healthy remember, so don't annoy me!*

I slip under the flow of water and consciously brush all those negative thoughts down the plug-hole.

How about a nice breakfast? You deserve it, says the voice. *Maybe a little old fry-up, followed by croissants? Ah go on, it's Saturday.*

Go away, I retaliate, *I am not listening, I'm not listening, I'm not listening.*

I lather up the soap and smooth the suds over my body, delighted with curves that are beginning to emerge after months of food restriction. The water pummels down my neck and my back. I arch to reach all those difficult places.

What are we going to have for dinner? says the voice. *How about a nice succulent roast beef with all the trimmings?*

I can feel my mouth watering, my tummy rumbling and can almost smell those potatoes, crispy on the outside and fluffy on the inside, roasted in goose fat, of course.

I scrub the shampoo through my hair and make a shopping list in my head. *Pâté to start, then I'll need cream and butter and I'll go to the market, get some nice cheese and a rhubarb tart. It is Saturday after all. Oh, and I'll need a good bottle of wine to wash that down.*

Yippee! says the voice, *I'm going to be fed. I'm starving. Yummy, yummy, lip-smacking delicious, fattening gourmet food at last!*

I turn off the shower and suddenly all is quiet. I come back to reality with a jolt and dry myself on the rough towel, determined to wipe away those cravings, trying to come to terms with the guilt of even thinking about it. Dressed, I plod down to the kitchen, take the skimmed milk out of the fridge and put on the porridge.

And so my eternal war with the Middle-Age Spread goes on. Oh well, it's OK to dream, I suppose!

Paula Lahiff

Musings from outside the (age) bracket

I mourn the loss of my seven and a half inches, too close for comfort to a whopping twelve per cent of my heyday height. I look back in anger at that earlier mid-life slice when I could have taken steps to forestall the ravages of the osteoporosis accountable for my dwindling stature. A less punitive austerity diet might then have sufficed, and a more rigorous exercise programme might have been implemented.

I often speak with wry humour of the onset of my puberty. I hated the dress my grandmother had made, its gaudy multi-hues, its hard, cold wiriness. Mainly I abhorred the gathers in the front waistline. "They'll add to it," she insisted, giving the seam a forward tug. However, my pleas fell on deaf ears. The world is unfairly divided: hordes of all classes, creeds and kinds are given more mammary largesse than they know what to do with, while others' hormones fail to fulfil their function. For the duration of my youth, 'shaped' bodices were the rage and flattered the well-endowed, but empty pouches wobbled and quivered on less fortunate chests.

I look back with resentment at a slice of my pre-teen life, when a slip of my foot a-top a damp clay ditch, a careering down its grassy slope, a thwack of my tail end on the harder field below, resulted in an unacknowledged and untreated injury which possibly occasioned the kyphosis that materialised a few years later. Including this account of the mishaps may be justified by the drastic effects of a hunched back on all my ensuing life slices: its unsightliness; its mis-shaping of garments; its engendering of mental and emotional problems, aches, pains and weakness.

I look back with gratitude on the life-slice I spent as a pupil of the Sligo Ursuline Nuns. I appreciate the boon they were to me and assure all and sundry that, 'sure as every

April turns to May', they were out there in a class of their own. Their influence did not wane even after I had bitten off that pleasant mid-life slice.

The wedded state was never my goal. I took my pre-Confirmation religious instruction seriously and St. Paul set the marriage bar too high. I wasn't resigned to submit to the requirements, nor willing to live outside them. Oh! I know that, had I fallen in love, the holy man in question would have gone out the window feet first. There was one sad consequence. I wanted a little moo-moo and a woman unaided cannot manage a cow. That apart, a husband is handy, unsurpassed for chopping wood, clearing the U-bend, hanging pictures…

Skill with the scissors and the Singer was a boon. Cleverly crafted seams were re-sewn, excess fabric ruthlessly slashed or deftly folded to give a modicum of padding, or to be at hand in case of 'turning' or as replacement for 'handing down'. Though still yearning for a bust, I look back with gratitude at the era that brought blissful relief in the guise of loose, non-figure-hugging dresses.

I ponder with amazement at how a group at 'Delia's Bridge Holiday' took me, a non-buff, under their wing and ensured I had a suitable seat at dinner. I wasn't at a loose end anytime. They even persuaded me to shuffle about on the dance floor while they danced all around. I'd like to assure my Rheumatology Team that I was very cautious, took precautions not to put a foot wrong, was amply cared for by the zealots and didn't attempt the gyrations portrayed by the lady on the Prolia booklet.

With no major illnesses or misfortunes to contend with, having an education and a profession, there has been nothing in my own life, or that of my family or extended family, to invoke lurid media headlines. I have to acknowledge that, taking one thing with another, I have been dealt a reasonable hand of cards.

Mary McEnroy

The journey

We have all come together

In sorrow and in pain

United in our battle

To reclaim our lives again

Nobody understands us

They look at us in awe

They do not comprehend us

Or our feelings that are raw

It's great to have the freedom

Without needing to explain

Just what our hopes and fears are

To make life whole again

Just as there's life hereafter and

Though things will never be the same

We have started on our journey and

Thank God there's light again

September 2011 – the turning point

MB

The road continues   **Mary Kearns**

The moment of truth

Sally looked at herself in the bathroom mirror, "Sometimes I think you do it on purpose," she told herself. "There I was having a lovely dream and you have to bring in the I'm falling, falling, falling ending again." She shook her toothbrush at the face in the mirror then grinned at herself. Reflecting on a brief moment of self revelation she realised she had been doing it again. Talking to herself or was it herself talking to another self living inside her? If there was another self was there only one or were there lots of them? The thought of many selves intrigued her and she fell to wondering who they might be.

At odd moments during the day she found herself, or was it one of the others, noting down different names for some of the selves. Negative very active: Positive very low key: Creative in spasms: Critical very active: Judgemental of self and others very active. By the evening she had quite an extensive list. As she mulled it over, she came to the conclusion that she needed to lighten up and become a more rounded person. Where was the fun, enjoyment, kindness, gentleness and interaction in a helpful way with others, that she so admired?

With a nod she determined that things were going to change. She started a list of the things she found fun and enjoyed and how long it had been since she last did them. She was amazed to find how sparse the list was and the length of time since she had done any of them. How had it happened? As she reflected, she saw that most of the things had ceased when John had died. Retreating into her shell she had unthinkingly allowed herself to lose her zest for life. Cutting herself off from couples they had known as friends together. Not attempting to make new ones.

When was the last time she had asked anyone round for a meal or a cuppa? That was what she had enjoyed most, the meals, the talk around the table touching on so many interesting things. These were what she really missed; now she thought about it.

Now back to the list. Kindness and gentleness. Certainly being more positive would help here. As would being less sharp-tongued. Zip lip and engage brain before blurting out critical remarks must be the order of the day. She was suddenly tired, putting the lists aside she told herself, "I'll work on this again tomorrow." As she finished brushing her teeth she said to the face in the mirror, "See what you have started. We are all in for some exciting times. Only the Lord knows where it will all end." She grinned and went to bed.

Elizabeth Dowd

Vision of a boatman series 1   Patricia Curran-Mulligan

Moments

There are moments
when I don't feel the sweep

of growing old; my skin supple
the wall of my stomach silk –

like wet glaze dipped
on a biscuit fired plate.

My profile from the neck down
all drifts and hollows

the blueness of distant hills
on the peaks of my breasts.

There is no thinning of hair
no fine tracery of veins

on the ridge of my cheek –
just a memory of lips

brushing lightly
over that landscape.

In other moments
I mark out boundaries

tattoo those places
where red veins rise

like worms to the surface
of damp soil

trace out an autumn of dappled
shade on my arms and legs

wake to a new birth groan –
flesh folding over and over.

Olivia Kenny McCarthy

A Feeling slice of mid-life

"It is so many years before one can believe enough in what one feels
even to know what the feeling is"

WB Yeats
Autobiographies (A 105), 1955

This theme encompasses an eclectic rainbow of feelings, ranging from fear and rejection to love and exuberance. Most are expressed in poetry, a format often used to articulate those thoughts and feelings most difficult to put into words. This theme beautifully encapsulates so many sensitive, humorous and powerful images in diverse styles of verse and prose. These include: how it feels to love, to have "found paradise", to be in tune with "perfect harmonies".

This slice of mid-life encompasses how it feels to mourn, to be abandoned or to be trapped "in the cage of my life" or "the quicksand of sadness". Yet there are over-riding feelings of optimism and joy: "I want to do my jelly belly-dance", "Never wilder, never more full of grace", never more lucky "to take in a panorama of endless sky."

In expressing our feelings we open up our heart and souls. Describing our feelings and sharing them with others involves courage and trust, both in oneself and in others; but the process also cultivates confidence and strength. There is no doubt that the breadth and depth of feelings expressed in this book will be shared by many other women, not just in mid life, but at any age. After all, age is just a number.

Maureen

Surviving

(for LB)

Two deer on a sloping hillside,
Silent in the slanting sun,
Smell suddenly the danger smell.
Then – stand and stare.

Then leg it
To that secret place,
Where you've turned your clock back
Tick by tiny tick
To where the poets ply their trade
And rainbows arch the sky
With broken light and promises of fortune.
Sweet music serenades
The ripening berries and the lazy bees.

There,
Skin is smooth
And needs no cut and thrust
To dig the canker out.
There, no bloody bits are choking in
Your tide of life, your rough and tumble.

Oh how you legged it!
There was no plan, no plot, no ploy,
Just run and hide and plug the tears

Till sanity came creeping back,
Tick by tiny tock

And left one closed-up whitening scar
Your only witness
To the jagged fear of darkness
On that far-off sunny hill.

Susan O'Keefe

I want jam on it!

Today, I want to be apple jelly
pink-cheeked
perfumed
spreadable
looking out of my jar.

I want to do my jelly, belly-dance
all sweetness and light –
firm enough to set
myself down on soft soda bread,
wobbly enough to soak
into your taste buds,
tangy enough
to be remembered
with delight.

Anne O'Connell

Mammy's brown bread   **Sue McNamee**

On being fifty

I will fly my birthday like a flag,
high above the galleon of my being,
fluttering symbol, gallant gaudy rag.

I will not let my *siúlóir* spirit drag,
instead I will regard it as a freeing.
I will fly my birthday like a flag.

My life's experiences gathered in a bag,
scraps glittering, jumbled out for seeing,
fluttering symbol, gallant gaudy rag.

I will not let self-righteous people nag,
instead I will go carolling and gleeing,
I will fly my birthday like a flag.

I'll wear bright colours though my shape might sag,
you'll not find me to diet gurus fleeing,
fluttering symbol, gallant gaudy rag.

Though I may cause conformist tongues to wag,
I will not stunt myself agreeing.
I will fly my birthday like a flag,
fluttering symbol, gallant gaudy rag.

Carol Wilson

A woman who has so many things to do

After A Woman Who ...... Drawings by Rebecca Miller

She gets up in the morning and goes to the door,
She walks in the dog dirt that's there on the floor.
Why did she let that young pup in the house?
More work than he's worth – feed, de-flea, de-louse.

Breakfast is next – oh no, there's no time!
It's starting to rain and there's sheets on the line.
The kids are all up now, looking for clothes,
But they're all on the line, now she's tense and it shows.

The traffic is heavy, rag week in full swing,
The meeting has started, her boss glares – worst thing!
Where are the notes that she copied last night?
Sitting at home, where she worked by the light!

Lunch time means shopping – the supermarket kind,

Milk, loaves and fishes, now where's the short line?

A tooth hurts, but dentists take time – can't afford!

How can young people complain that they're bored?

A walk would be nice, but there's more work in that,

There's kids to be dressed, and they must bring the cat!

So it's easier give in, and get started on dinner,

But mother rings half way, and she's always the winner.

There's a house to be tidied, and lunch to be made,

How can they talk of 'me-time', for God's sake?

The bathroom needs cleaning, the towels need to go,

She's got to learn somewhere, sometime, to say no!

Deirdre Cox

Early mid-life gifts

Never clearer, never more confused

Never happier, never more easily moved

Never fuller, never more gloriously hollow

Never lighter, never more solid

Never brighter, never more aware of the dark

Never hotter, never more aware of the spark

Never surer, never more shaky

Never emptier, never more sated

Never securer, never more grateful

Never busier, never more still

Never easier, never less eager to please

Never graver, never more of a tease

Never looser, never more fully alive

Never calmer, never more brain-fried

Never wilder, never more full of grace

Never freer, never more place and space

Never better, never more bold

Never younger

Never, no never,

Less ready for

'old'.

Bríd Brady

Essence of womanhood   Laura Bell

Three chords and the truth

One of the places I would love to visit is Nashville, Tennessee. I hear it's hot though. I don't 'do hot' much anymore.

It might have been those earliest experiences my sisters and I had of being regularly plonked on a West Cork beach to broil to a nice all-over brown. Tender baby skin protested and industrial quantities of Nivea were needed to soothe that glowing two-bar electric fire feeling before bed. Or maybe it was the insatiable hunger for sun and tan that found me basting in my teens, unwittingly daring the sun to come and do its damage. I didn't realise that being nut-brown was no protection until I chanced to meet some Aussie girls in Morocco. They told me about their alarming rates of 'immigrant' skin cancer and of their beach health promotion campaigns. At least it explained their hilarious legionnaire style hats. In time I reached that stage when my personal body thermometer took on a life of its own, progressing rapidly way beyond initially 'welcome' floods of warmth. No amount of re-framing it into power surges gets away from the sheer nuisance of on/off duvets, cardigans and inopportune sweat fests. Now I get heat rashes ranging from mildly tingling to tearing itchy and sore when I show myself to a hot sun. Only my dermatologist can look without flinching.

So given this discomfort with hot places, why Nashville you might be wondering? I should say it's not just Nashville – even though the 'Grand Ole Opry' is only nine miles from the centre of town. If I were to walk all the way from Boulder to Birmingham like Emmylou, it would be a five-state ramble at least. I would have to take in Baton Rouge for sure, through the east Texas back-roads and nip down along the Gulf Coast Highway, maybe going back to Greenville or Jackson. The names all resonate powerfully from the many wonderful country music songs I am still growing up with. I am not sure why country songs don't seem to lend themselves as easily to Irish place names; it should be as easy to build a story around a woman's struggle in Tubbercurry as Tallahassee. But the southern states are where country music is reputed to have had its beginnings in the 1920s, taking its simple forms and harmonies from immigrant folk traditions, African and cowboy roots. Some might be tempted to ask why anyone in their right mind would want to pay attention to country music, when there are symphonies, jazz, tangos and operas to listen to. Or why someone given to nasty heat rashes would seek out the cauldron that is the Southern States to check out the places in those songs?

There are many varied genres within country music and I love it, from the heart-rending 'hurting' ballads with perfect harmonies to the slick tight sassy bluegrass sounds, to name but two. But country music for me is arguably at its best when it captures life's ordinary 'earthy' moments. Like the woman home from a hard day's work, having gone to considerable trouble to get ready for a romantic evening, despairingly asking of her disinterested beer-guzzling partner, "Did I shave my legs for this?" Or another falling for the clearly unavailable protagonist wistfully ending her chorus with, "You've got a lot of balls, you don't even care .... wish I could grow a pair." There is definitely room in there for a sweating song. I just might have to write it.

As Howard Harlan, a prolific country music songwriter now buried in Nashville city cemetery, put it, "Country music is three chords and the truth." Right on, Howard. I too am searching for the truth.

Maire O'Gara and David Pierce

Mary Roche

Just because

Just because.... it wasn't real
Does not mean .... I did not believe

Just because.... the chains are gone
Does not mean .....I savour freedom

Just because.... it was all I had
Does not mean .....it was all I wanted

Just because.... I suspected
Does not mean .....I wanted to be right

Just because.... I was afraid to look
Does not mean ..... I am not brave

Just because.... I found my courage
Does not mean ..... there is no pain

Just because.... my fears were founded
Does not mean ..... I was not shocked

Just because.... you lied and cheated
Does not mean ..... I never loved you

Just because.... I know the truth
Does not mean ..... I don't love you

Just because.... you covered up
Does not mean ..... I don't understand

Just because.... I was right
Does not mean ..... I feel better

Just because.... the pain is piercing
Does not mean ..... I am feeble

Just because.... I trusted you
Does not mean ..... I am naive

Just because.... you led me on
Does not mean ..... I was not willing

Just because.... I was willing
Does not mean ..... I should be scorned

Just because.... you call me names
Does not mean ..... they don't hurt

Just because.... you know my weakness
Does not mean ..... I should have to hide

Just because.... the truth is ugly
Does not mean ..... there was no beauty

Just because.... you abused me
Does not mean ..... I don't miss you

Just because.... you broke my heart
Does not mean ..... I won't forgive you

Just because.... you say I am the same
Does not mean ..... I am

Anonymous

Hands

Dear Hands,

I write to you both collectively as I know you each depend on the other and work better when you work as a team. Sometimes one of you needs encouragement as you feel a little weak but, rather than put one of you on the spot and single you out, I want to encourage you both today in the work that you do.

You could be identical twins except for the birthmark on you, left hand. Never feel this is a defect or flaw, but rather that it makes you stand out so that people can have a conversation with you. Perhaps your experience of life might help someone come to terms with an issue they might have.

My first recollection of you both was as a child when people would remark "Oh, you have piano fingers." This remark still reminds me of a road we travelled for a short time, and to my lasting sorrow we did not go far enough. I appreciate you both for being with me for so long as I look at others with parts missing, fingers no longer there, bones out of shape and some too stiff to use. Just recently, I bought my friend a purse that had an opening device where she could slide out her money so that the shop assistant could pick up the coins for her. Some years ago, another younger friend could not grasp a cup due to a life-threatening illness. Oh, how I appreciate you both.

Looks are not important. You have been with me all these years and have been helping me be me – able to write a letter, lift the phone to communicate and call a friend, cook a meal for family, friends or even a stranger. How faithful you both have been. Some people love gardening, others photography and so on, but crafts have been my thing. How could I do without you? I shudder to think. You have been there in the middle of the night when sleep escapes me and I sit making cards. You are more than friends – you are my mentors and therapists. I make no apology for repeating these words. How could I have done without you both?

The visit to Romania was a very special one. I wondered how I could communicate as I did not have the language. Little did I know, when I packed some bottles, how you would come into your own. Maria came to live in the Home and I had the privilege of being there as she left the dilapidated cottage she lived in. She was blind. She was distraught at leaving her only home but could no longer live in such conditions. You were the heroes of the day, as for some hours you sat and held her hands, and ministered love to her by gently rubbing her hands and feet with oil. She kept murmuring "domni, domni." It was the first physical touch she had felt in a very long time. She would often ask about you when we left and I was so pleased you met her again on a recent visit. How eagerly she touched you both and tenderly smoothed over your skin with her warm hands. I got a shock when, two days after our visit, I heard that Maria had died suddenly. I remember how pleased I was that someone had taken a picture of you both, clasped in Maria's hands.

As I clasp you both together now in prayer, I thank God for the gift He has given me of you both. Please remember on days when you feel tired and discouraged, the things you have been able to do. Be glad, and remember that, whatever the future holds, as long as you are together you can accomplish twice as much.

Take care of each other.

Margaret Colvin

Your side of the wardrobe

I cull dust
from emptiness,
palm specks,
stare at years
of loneliness.

I spill tears
that moisten
motes of memory,
wash our time
in drops that shine.

Jean Folan

Labyrinth

Thirty years ago, I owned a sea garden. 'Panoramic views over the golf course', the estate agent's blurb had said. There was a green patch of straggly grass, a few stunted conifers and a rickety fence, behind which there was a tumbledown boundary wall and a thicket of brambles and nettles. It was a garden to be looked out of rather than looked at, dominated by Knocknarea and the sand dunes, with a horizon of sea that stretched from Mayo to Donegal. I thought it was the loveliest place on earth.

Now the views are blocked on most sides and my garden is enclosed. A house gable obscures all but a sliver of Knocknarea. There is a street where the field behind used to be. I can only see an inch of sea if I stand on tippy-toes on the step of the shed at the top of the garden. But, in a book I once read, I learnt that the word paradise means 'enclosure'.

In the top quarter of the garden, between the rowan tree and the elderberry, beyond the rambling rose and beside the statue of Buddha, I have built a labyrinth. It is 19 feet wide. The outer layer is of large stones that were once part of a dwelling house. Inside these, the smaller dividing stones are pieces of elsewhere, picked up lovingly one-by-one on other journeys. Internal paths are gravel and stone, all recycled or reclaimed from other garden projects.

A labyrinthine journey is a surprisingly long one. Even within this small space, it is a two minute walk to the centre, crunching along the paths, meeting old favourites among the stones. There are no wrong turnings. It is impossible to get lost. Concentric circles loop around, but appear slightly skewed, because each one joins to the next layer. Overall, the shape is not unlike that of a human brain, though sometimes it reminds me of a big, ornate tree. As the paths wind forward and back on themselves, they take me, now in a clockwise direction, now anticlockwise. This journey is said to take one to the centre of self.

As I approach the heart of the labyrinth, the corners are tighter. When I arrive in the central space and pause there, I feel that I have reached the still point at the centre of the universe. In here is my collection of special stones – crystals, the unique artwork of the universe – in mauve, brown, pink, grey and clear colours. There is a beautiful piece of Achill amethyst that was given to me as a present and a beach stone with the word Om inscribed on it in fossil strokes. My own personal favourite is a dull grey stone with a small white mouth, inside of which are a myriad tiny, clear quartz crystals with one pure, perfect amethyst at its core. It speaks to me of worlds within worlds and infinite possibility.

My vistas haven't shrunk, they have expanded. Among these ancient stones, I have found paradise.

Órfhlaith Ní Chonaill

Labyrinth   Órfhlaith Ní Chonaill

On reaching 60

What matters now is the process,
The learning, the doing,
The almost-getting there,
The being with friends,
The here and now,
Today.

Gone is the worry of the what-if's,
The what-might-be's,
The tomorrows and all their needs,
The finished products,
Perfection.

What matters now is how to strive,
How to live each new day,
To love and be loved,
To give and to receive
How to deal with each new moment
And not over-dwell on the past,
And how to move silently and gently towards
Tomorrow.

Helen Coleman

I'll not pause

Hello this is me
Do not call me dear
This sultry woman is not
going to pause
The possibilities are
endless and set to enthral
The London Eye beckons
with reckless appeal
I'll shine a light on
what's important and not
Buy shop made jam and
pretend it's mine
I will travel down under
and party at length
Smile at strangers and put on a bet

I will tiptoe through the sand
Spend hours chasing waves
I'll wear bright colours
And take part in a reel
I'll let no day pass
without an event
Meet up with friends at
the toss of a hat
Toast prosecco and not green tea
Meet at the spa and shout hurrah
Hello this is me
and I'm going far.

Josephine Feeney

Menopause moments

Here I am at last
where my mother used to be
hot flushes and night sweats
much worse than puberty.

I never saw it coming
for it just crept up on me
and took me by surprise
at the age of fifty-three.

There's benefits you know
'cos there's no more bloody flow
no painful cramps no PMS
no waiting in distress.

Though I wish there was a way
I could put it all on hold
to stop the strangest feeling
that I am getting old.

What with osteoporosis
psychosis and neurosis
and HRT to set us free
but side affects – atrocious!

So let me see if I can find
a way to set us free
to join the human race again
with newfound liberty.

To hell with all the agony
let's celebrate this life
yes, it's the mid-life crisis
let's put an end to strife.

Angela Feeney

Dark

Sometimes I am a coward in the dark,

My home creaks unsettlingly as I wake from sleep.

The imagined intruder?

The cooker left on?

The wiring .... faulty?

What's that smell?

Did I blow out the candle?

Unplug the iron?

Is the smoke alarm working?

Who's outside? Surely the dog would bark?

Thump, thump. I hear my heart.

God, my heart!

How long would the ambulance take?

Would it be too late?

Don't be stupid.

Get up.

Turn on a light.

What was all that about?

Glad that's over.

Fluff up the pillows

      drift off

            sweet dreams.   **Catherine Byrne**

Unknown

Kim Doherty

Love

How could you invade my every living cell
And make my life such a waking hell?
Each step that I took, each breath that I drew
Made me aware I was invaded by you.

My head it was dizzy, my eyes were a blur,
I quivered within, my voice was a slur.
My eyes are all weepy, I can't sleep at night,
Every moment of the day, I don't feel quite right.

You're there in the morning, you're there when I dream,
You're there in my limbs and in my blood stream.
You take away my focus, my mind is askew.
Are you my love? No, you're only the flu!

Rose Holmes

16 September 1964 – 16 December 2009

Submitted by Olive Henry (sister)

The Leaving

The decision was yours.
  I could only hope you
    Would change your mind.

Twice I have faced
  This situation.
    Twice it had worked well.

Now was the third time.
  You said "Enough, I cannot
    Go through it again".

So I wait, will you change
  Your mind? The date is fixed.
    It passes, still you say "No."

Just 14 days later the call comes
  You have left me without a word.
    All I can say is "Go in peace."

Elizabeth Dowd

Tomorrow

Oh to escape – just for a day – just to be alone!
Where to? Perhaps to a lonely Atlantic beach,
to hear the surf and feel the sea spray on my face.
To see the waves, sparkling like jewels in the sun,
wash and break on sand and stone.
If I could stay there until the red sun sinks
like a flame into the dark of the sea
and feel the shade of night comforting me.
But today I must stay in the cage of my life,
surrounded by bodies and lonesomeness.
Tomorrow – maybe tomorrow .....

Ann Bradshaw

A new dawn   **Val Robus**

Lucky few

Some people know what it's like ... by Rita Ann Higgins

Some people know what it's like
to sit on a bench at the end of their springtime garden
and hear the arriving geese from far off
to watch the horizon as they appear over the brow of the hill
in their lines of an imperfect moving V
to feel the downdraft of their wings as they pass overhead
to follow their flight determinedly northwards
hooting and honking and thumping their feathered muscle fans.

Some people know what it's like
to walk the long beach on a still grey autumn day
to the sound track of the listless waves
to breathe in the silence and calm
then hear the punctuation splash of water shattered
looking seawards, catch the humps and flicked tails
of a pod of dolphins crossing the bay
to stop as if time itself has stopped and pan your head
slowly right to left in a hundred and eighty degrees
following their performance passing just offshore
and there's no one else around.
It is a private show.
Just you and the quiet sea and the dolphins.

Some people know what it's like

to pilot a canoe along the estuary on a summer Sunday

going far out into mid-stream and lie back flat, balanced with the paddle,

to hear the sounds of flies and seagulls

and the flop of fish jumping near the boat

to take in a panorama of endless sky, the mountain shapes of landmass

and shimmering slivers of light bouncing on the water

to look to shore and see otters running among rocks

and pass close eyeball to eyeball with a heron

poised at its catching vantage point and not prepared to move.

But most people on this crowded planet

walk and sit and stamp and talk and stand and gather.

They jostle and rush and push and shove and squash.

They argue and shout to be heard above the noise of all the others.

They flail around in their maelstrom of urban living.

Most people in our seven thousand millions will never

lie back on a canoe floating seawards in the sunshine

or sit alone in a quiet garden and feel a bird migration pass

or walk an empty beach in the company of dolphins.

Out of seven billion, we are the lucky few.

Mary Manandhar

Worn

Swirling, twirling mystery of fire
Reminds me of storms I cannot face alone.
Suddenly, drenched in terror,
A tidal wave of emotions engulfs me.
I had a jumper like that...
Powerless.

Were there any bounds?
Did I have a choice?
I feel directionless
Desperate.
I had a jumper like that...

Afraid to feel, I learned to touch.
Struggling.
You did not catch me when I fell.
Tears come up from my body
Long, hot,
Yearning for that huge blanket of love.
You did not catch me when I fell.

Tell me truth,
Tell me what is behind your eyes?
Are you broken?

You contain a terrifying darkness,
Growing more frantic, I see.
Childhood simplicity it was not,
A quicksand of sadness trapped me,
Your ugly glory – loud.
You leave me complex, fragile.
I had a jumper like that ...
It's worn.

Mary CH

Better days?

My God, I'm such a wreck.

Is there any part of me that

Has not seen better days?

Parts taken out

And parts put in

False hip, womb gone

Cataracts removed

Muscles bucked

Hair dyed

Tummy tucked.

At least I still have my teeth!

And my laughter lines

And my eyesight

And my humour

And my dreams

And my hopes

And my smile

And my love

Paula Lahiff

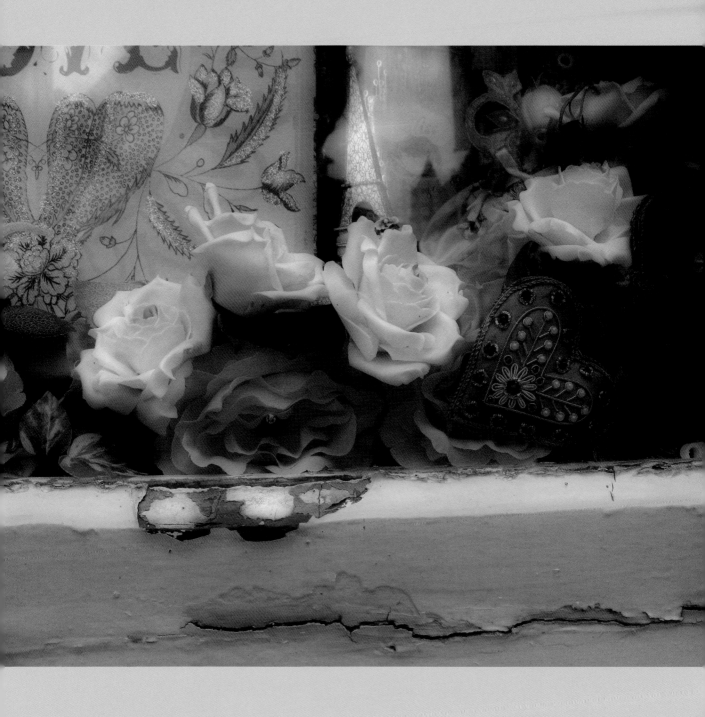

A Loving slice of mid-life

"That Love is all there is,
Is all we know of Love"

Emily Dickinson
Complete Poems, 1924.
Part Five: The Single House CXII

The theme of loving has been at the core of numerous submissions. Although the book has been divided into themes, the images created by the poetry, prose and art often transcend them. By its very nature, love is enmeshed in the other three themes. This, of course, mirrors the reality of life, where the ebb and flow is a constant overlapping of interweaving themes. Love is an enormously powerful emotion; writers throughout the ages have tried, with varying results, to describe its many guises and layers. This theme encompasses a wonderful and varied selection of pieces which explore the broad spectrum of love in its myriad forms.

From physical love to comfortable love, from the search for love to the loss of love, intimate love is described with humour and poignancy. The special bond between mother and child is captured in the love of a mother for her child and the love of a daughter for her mother. We share the magic and joy of being a grandmother and glimpse the special love for an eccentric auntie. Women have the capacity to love and be loved in so many different ways. This section of the book is a vibrant mid-life testament to that love.

Maureen

7

Dear Kate

Dear Kate,

I have been reflecting on life before your arrival and I realise that nothing and everything has changed. Nothing has changed in that I face the same challenges, do the same housework, go to work each day and play catch-up at the weekends. Yet everything has changed since the day you were born. I remember seeing you for the first time, this perfect little baby, and feeling an overwhelming love for my precious granddaughter.

I remember feeling a tremendous and protective love for your mother and your uncles, but this feeling for you is different. Maybe it's because I was so busy rearing my own children that I don't remember experiencing this wonder and awe that I feel when I look at you. My friends who have become grandparents before me always say it's a special blessing and now I really understand what they mean. When I look at you and you gaze solemnly back and then break into your tremendous smile, my heart melts.

No matter how busy or challenging my day is, I get this wonderful happy feeling when I look at the screen saver on my phone and see your smiling face. You have changed my life irrevocably and I appreciate how lucky I am to be a grandparent. I look forward each day to hearing all about you and to seeing you at weekends. I am truly blessed to have you in my life, especially at this time when many things are changing, to give me a new perspective on the years to come.

God bless you always.
Nanna.

Moya Wilson

Eva in February

In the mud and rushes of Ballisodare Bay,
With the light glittering on the sand-filled pools,
You laughed out loud
At the unexpected softness of the seeds,
Their lightness in the brittle three o'clock sun.

As you pulled them from their staff,
Their life-enhancing fluff drove them
To settle on your muddied trousers
Where they fastened without prospect,
While you shredded more of the velvet brown pods,
Turning sunshine to a sudden silky snow.

Enchanted by the flurry,
Now, tarred and feathered by your
Sunday afternoon tangle with nature,
You came home.
Guilty of no offence save
The spreading of life
In a moment of laughter.

Susan O'Keefe

Slices

Mama has warm hands. She holds my small ones as we walk down the back lanes together. I see colours on the clotheslines. Red, blue, yellow. Mama is fat. Not her face, her belly. My baby sister is sleeping in the pram at home, a holy medal pinned to the hood. Now we are turning around to go back. We meet a dog and I am afraid, but Mama picks me up.

"Shush, shush, it's fine, he won't hurt you."

We go in the back door and Mama puts on the kettle. She takes the soda bread from the oven and the big green knife from the drawer. "A slice of bread for my best girl," she says.

I love Mama. Soon I will be three years old.

The orange juice tastes strong and sweet as we pass the cup around. Everyone is thirsty and tired. It is a hot July afternoon and we've walked a long way. There are eight of us. Dada and Mama and us six children. I am the eldest. The baby is still in nappies and Mama carries him. He has big blond curls. I hold him while she cuts the sponge cake into pieces. She tries to make the slices all the same size.

"A slice for you, Elizabeth?" I am ten years old.

It is a breezy May morning. My face aches. I'm tired smiling. Now we sit at the top of the wedding table, all eyes upon my new husband and me. It is a small wedding, just the two families. I cannot swallow, so I don't eat. Then it is time to cut the cake. We are given a big knife by the hotel staff. We pretend to cut, and smile, yet again. In the photos later we look like children. The staff bustles away cutting the cake into slices.

"A slice for you, Liz?" my new husband asks. I am twenty.

I made a train cake for his birthday. My son is three today and he grabs at the liquorice wheels with his plump little fingers. Mama leans across his shoulder to light the candles. There are seven children. A lot of noise. Someone spills juice while another child needs the toilet. Mama helps with that and then we sing "Happy Birthday" for the third time, just so he can blow the candles again. We cut the cake and pass it around.

"A slice for you, Mum?" I ask. I am thirty.

Mama is seventy today. We are all together celebrating. She sits at the top of the table and the waitress says, "Your mama is the queen."
I know she is. The queen of hard work, patience and love. Dada is gone now, as is one brother. We eat a lovely meal, and then a cake is brought in. "Happy Birthday," we sing. Mama cuts the cake. It is her last party.

"A slice for everyone?" she says. I am forty.

My sister and I walk in Regents Park, London. Orange, red and purple flood our senses from the autumn trees and flowerbeds. I am over to see a medical consultant. We speak of love, brothers and sisters, Mama. We walk together like we did as children. I am getting tired. We sit at a small garden café.

"Will we try a slice of beetroot cake with our coffee?" I ask my sister.

"Let's share it," she replies.

We share the slice. I am fifty.   **Elizabeth Fox**

Islanders

In this place the people
are stranded islanders,
trapped within glens created
by ice age volcanoes
and scree that slid inevitably
towards the cold, boiling sea;
the island tossed and hurled,
until it came, unwilling,
to join the rest.

Dogged in their difference,
the stranded people held fast
to the small heat inside themselves,
not quenched by cold
nor the pull of land,
land whose voice is heard
in rain dripping from leaves through
rocky clefts
to bubbling rivers below.

I sit upon the severed causeway,

contemplate my island self,

this forced separation.

Though you speak of tumult and its testimony,

black basalt,

I am at peace here amid the wind,

the spray-crested waves,

and know that it is you

who is waiting

as I make my way home.

Maeve MacDermott

Blue (Seal Cove)   **Mary Kearns**

Is beag an dealg a dhéanann sileadh

She watched him leave in the morning as he did every morning, half an hour before her, to beat the traffic. Up at 7.30, tea and toast, wash hair and shower, grab briefcase – regular as clockwork, nothing unusual there. Boring in its predictability after twenty years of marriage. But there was one big difference. He had forgotten to kiss her goodbye.

Such an insignificant omission, true, but there had to be a reason. Thoughts chased themselves in circles around her head, unbidden, as she cleared away the dishes on autopilot. Maybe he was just tired? A little later than usual? Pressure of work? Something worrying him? Just after a bad dream, perhaps? Was it the beginning of the end? Had he simply forgotten? How could he forget her? Could there be another woman? Was there a communication crisis unknown to her? When was the last time they had been intimate? Worse still, were they drifting into apathy? Had he stopped loving her? Would they be just good friends from now on? Where was the passion? Had they allowed themselves to become creatures of habit? Did he simply not care anymore? Or was he deliberately ignoring her? Had she missed something? Had she forgotten to ask him about some sniffle or symptom? Was it his birthday? Surely she couldn't have become that thoughtless!

She told herself not to be so silly, grabbed her coat, got into her car, came back three times to put the cat out, turn off the radio, and lastly, lock the door. She would have to focus! Enough of this nonsense! Such a simple incident! Forget it!

But what should she do about it? She couldn't just ignore it! Should she ring him? Or leave a message? Should she accuse him of ignoring her? Should she simply remind him that she loved him? Should she make a special effort this evening? Or ignore him until he asked her what was wrong? Or accuse him of losing interest, so he would hold her and reassure her? Maybe she should come home later than usual, just to worry him? Make him appreciate her a little bit more?

She jumped as the mobile on the car seat beeped. The little blue light flashed a message. All was right with the world again!

Deirdre Cox

Slim chance

Eliza, if ... by Christianne Balk

If she stayed in the city
If she stayed in that good job
She would be different now
If she never went there
If she was never captivated by the place
If she was never drawn to it, as though by a magnet.
If....

She would not have met him after all the years
If he also, was not captivated by the place
And went there, and stayed separately,
She would have missed this.
He would have missed this.

They were both drawn from the same city, separately,
They found each other in this place.
It was a slim chance.

Catherine Byrne

If

Eliza, if ... by Christianne Balk

If I had not met you

If I could have been me

If I did what I had wanted then

If I did not always put myself second to your needs

If I had told you no, I need my freedom still, I need to find me

I could have been free to say my mind to you,

Give myself the freedom to be me

If I had not always listened to my elders,

Those older important people who were always being so critical of who I am

If I could have been me then

I could have been free to say my mind to you

But that was then

If I loved you then, I did not know love

If I met you now would it be like then?

For now is different to then

If I loved you then, I love you still

For I know me now

The me of then is still here with the me I am now.

Breege Fox

Happy anniversary

On a warm autumn day
you said "I do"
and took a giant leap of faith,
no safety net
no back-up plan
no doubts
that 7 months of love was time enough
for certainty.

It all began on Platform 2 as I recall:
strangers waiting for a train
who found each other in a random queue
as lovers do in films
when fate is sealed by chance
in a momentary glance that spans eternity.

We boarded the train at Glasgow Central
swaying side by side to the rhythm of the rails
rocking back and forth to the heartbeat of the track
fuelled by a love that was never turning back
on a train that will rattle on forever.

Hurtling through time,
the years like stations passing in a blur
of life and love
like a landscape in 40 shades of green,
the tapestry of subtle tones felt
only by our hearts
and memories seen
only through our eyes
reflect the changing seasons as they fly.

We've been derailed and back on track
through darkest tunnels bleak and black
then into sunlight brighter still
with hopes and dreams yet to fulfil
and love that's stronger than before
that guides us through another door
on that train that will rattle on forever.

On a warm autumn day
I said "I do"
and took a giant leap of faith with you
which all began on Platform 2,
and I would jump again today
and twice as high
and know that love will last until I die,
for every day my journey starts
and ends with you,
so ask me now
that I may say again today

"I do, I do, I do
    love you,
        Martin Howley."

Maureen Howley

A time to stare   **Helen Coleman**

Love in free verse

Would that I could pen you the perfect love poem,
A graceful sonnet, romantic, à la Shakespeare.

My fingers seek the keys to heart-shaped words.
Yours linger still, caress my entire being.

Rhyme love with dove above. Too easy.
Pentameter, we shared five years. I am.

Try rhythm, our two hearts in unison,
Mine flutters, yours ceased in fibrillation.

Plagiarise, love's labour is never lost.
Love in free verse.

We are the perfect couplet:
                              uncoupled.

Jean Folan

Aunty Rose

Aunty Rose lived with her gay son and his older ex-army lover in a smart Art Deco apartment in a London tower block. She wandered into a room paying no attention to its function or the people in it. And sometimes, as if she could not remember why she had come in, she would wander right back out again.

She shuffled her small feet in oversize slippers across the shiny parquet floor. Her stockings would lie like concertinaed nylon hoops around her puffy ankles. She sat like a man with her knees wide apart so that her bloomer knickers were in full view to all. She never crossed her legs. She said that was unladylike. She smoked cigars every night on the balcony, with her gin and tonic *(large)* in her hand, holding animated conversations with the pigeons in the overhanging branches.

Rob and Simon lived their lives around her. They never mentioned her eccentricities, though sometimes they would laugh at her and say, "Oh Rose, you are a one!" Then just carry on with what they were doing, while Rose stood watching, munching on a Jacob's Cream Cracker. She latched firmly on to me when I went to stay.

"Robert is so kind," she would say. "He let me have his bedroom and he shares a bed with Simon. That's so kind, isn't it? They are such good friends."

I would nod and smile, and Rob would catch my eye and roll his about. 'Doesn't she know?' I thought.

I remember that the bathroom had no lock and, when I felt like a bit of peace from the constant opera music or Rose's endless sagas of chat, I retreated there for a long soak. But Rose would often follow me in, roll up her skirt, wriggle down her baggy stockings, pee on the toilet and stay there to chat some more.

'She's crazy,' I thought, but funny too, and tender. She would take my face in between her palms as she said goodnight and kiss each cheek lovingly. "There we go, pet. Another day. Sleep tight and don't let the bedbugs bite. And if they do, use dynamite!" I used to dread her face close up to mine – the smell of gin was overwhelming.

Aunty Rose liked to knit, crochet and sew, and make tapestries and embroideries. In every room, there were endless piles of fabric, and wool and cotton reels piled high. I remember the constant click-clack of needles. Simon tried hard not to be cross with her as she click-clacked once too often, or loudly, during a hushed and emotive aria.

"Another G and T, Rose?" he would ask, with resignation.

She didn't go out much. It wasn't really safe. She would forget the way and end up in Chalk Farm. When we did go out together, she would reminisce in great detail about her life as a young woman. Riding the red double-deckers into the West End, window-shopping in Piccadilly, meeting friends for tea in Lyons Corner Shop. Her eyes would shine bright. She didn't seem quite so crazy then, but clear and lucid as she set the scenes before me.

I could see, as she talked, the younger Rose. When she met and married my Uncle Jack. Before he signed up and joined the destroyers sent to protect England's lifeline of merchant shipping during the Atlantic blockades. Before she read the telegram about the enemy warship Graff Spee and him being torpedoed, lost at sea … "Her Majesty regrets." Before she took to the gin and raised her fatherless son, and knitted like the war and her life and her sanity depended on it.

I loved her, my mad Aunty Rose.

Mary Manandhar

Evening in Sligo

The light is long
on the floor of the countryside
on the road
woodbine and meadowsweet in the air.

Stands of loosestrife
tall grasses
great pillows of vetch
have taken their chance in newly-turned earth
have thrived in complained-about rain.

The evening is generous
I accept the invitation to walk in its silence
as if you were beside me.

Carmel Cummins

Untitled

Tessa Marsden

Enduring friendship

In memory of Karen (1952–2007) who died in Summerland, British Colombia, following a long battle with cancer

Dearest Bill, I write today what is in my heart as it is my only substitute for not being there in person, beside my dearest friend. I know you will judge when it is right to read this for Karen and I implicitly trust you with that decision.

27/11/07

My dearest Karen,

Time as we know it in our external world is suspended for me these last few weeks and days. I sit at my kitchen table, as so many times before, and think of you and the wonderful friendship we have enjoyed over the last 32 years. I always thought we were similar, you and I, in all that was dear to us – warm kitchens on cold days, family, friends and everywhere a circle of brightness and love, rooms suffused with colour, paintings and creative images.

All the time I travel this journey with you in my heart, over the years, words reaching out across the miles, entwined in time and space with one another.

Today the trees are a banner of colour in my garden, and I think of you and that gives me comfort. Today I picked a pink anemone in the garden swept by autumn, but bravely standing, and I think of you all the time at my side, my arms around you. I journey with you, my friend. I see your beautiful face, your fierce and awesome spirit in your tiny frame, and I know how blessed I am knowing you for such a long time. We have shared so much of ourselves over the years. We have crusaded like Joan of Arc for what we believed in. We have laughed, loved, sung, cried and celebrated our lives and our enduring friendship.

Each day I walk to the sea. Here, in the west of Ireland, I think of you as the waves roll in to the shore, the wild heron taking flight and our crazy red setter runs and runs chasing his dreams.

You are in my heart and soul and you inspire me as you have always done. I am there with you taking your hand, my friend. It is a beautiful thing, the journey of our friendship. We have loved and cared for one another, and at every life stage we have provided a soft place to fall for one another. We are there now together warming one another with love. I am blessed with your friendship. I know, as I have always known, that the more love you give away, the more the abundance of love you have in your life.

You have provided me with all the blessings, nurture and challenges for my journey. We have never been isolated, you and I. In my heart and soul I found my 'Anam Cara'.

I take your hand in your quiet room. I am there, I am there.

Ita Conroy

Single supplement

Carmel McNamee

Feelings

I had never imagined how

I could get through life without him.

I never had to do much constructive thinking.

I was always afraid of being left alone,

But life changes fast. Life changes in an instant.

Grief comes in waves, it blinds the eyes,

It blanks the mind, it numbs the senses.

But you have to pick up the pieces

And try and swim through

The next passage of your life.

A life that carries a world full of memories.

And you know he will still guide you

Through the difficult times, as he has always done.

Bridie McDermott

A significant birthday question answered

Soon I will be it, that 'Significant Birthday'. The *"Will you still need me, will you still feed me…?"* birthday. I don't know whether to rejoice I have actually made it this far or lament that it is all a slippery downward slope from here on in. In those heady Beatlemania days of the 1960s, I never even imagined that the day would come when I, myself, would be celebrating that birthday made so famous by the Fab Four.

Why do we celebrate birthdays at all, I wonder? "It's the day of your birth," I hear you say. It's a red letter day, a day to remember forever. But then there's your significant other's birthday too, and you try to match it up with your own. What sign of the zodiac is he? Is it compatible with your own? Is he older than you or younger?

Then your children come along and all their birthdays are added to the list. At first you remember the exact time of birth of each. Later, as you muddle your way through birthday parties and sticky buns and ice cream cakes in the shape of trains, and goody bags and bouncy castles, when THAT TIME comes around on the clock, you stop wiping a runny nose or a stinky bum and say to yourself, "Yes, it was about now that I gave that one last push!"

As time goes by, all the births seem to merge into one and when the lucky one whose birthday is being celebrated asks, "What time was I born Mam," you cross your fingers and make an educated guess. So, when I heard these familiar lyrics on the radio,

"When I get older losing my hair, many years from now,

Will you still be sending me a valentine, Birthday greetings, bottle of wine?",

it made me think of good memories of my teenage Beatle years and of other significant birthdays which finally brought me to this one.

My twenty-first birthday when I wore mini-skirts and false eyelashes and Dad gave me twenty-one pounds for keeping my promise of not smoking until that day. My twenty-fifth birthday – quarter of a century – when I got engaged and flashed my ring obviously under the noses of all those poor unfortunate single friends. My twenty-ninth birthday – oh yes, I'll stay twenty-nine forever – and then everything passes in a blur of child-rearing, home-making, financial gymnastics. My fortieth birthday arrives all too soon, it seems. Is it my imagination, or does time go by much faster as you get older? Life begins at forty – or as those thin and toned yummy mummies smugly say these days, 'forty is the new thirty'. My fiftieth birthday comes up and by this time I have already celebrated – if that is the right word – all the significant birthdays of my family as well. Age thirteen – a big milestone, a teenager! Sweet sixteen and never been kissed. I wonder! Eighteen years – key of the door – and it goes on and on.

On fiftieth birthdays – half a century – your children organise your birthday, usually a surprise party which you know all about, but have to feign total astonishment when your 'small family dinner' turns into one of those events where you look around at your friends and say to yourself, "Oh God, haven't they got SO OLD, put on SO MUCH WEIGHT. Is she DIVORCED now?" And you have to sit back and listen to in-depth stories of other people's children's academic achievements and their adventures in the Southern Hemisphere.

So when I come to celebrate my Significant Beatle Song Birthday in style, I will let everyone else do the work, sit back and enjoy it, and cluck like the proverbial mother hen when she has all her chicks around her, content in the knowledge that my Better Half will be, "*Doing the garden, digging the weeds, who could ask for more?*" and knowing that the answer to the question, "*Will you still need me, will you still feed me when I'm sixty-four?*" is most definitely YES.

Paula Lahiff

Pleasure

The pleasure of you.

Beautiful you.

Vibrant colours cross your naked pulsating body.

You, warm and clear.

You, desire.

I reach, I touch warm soft, supple skin.

You, dancing endlessly towards me.

The pleasure of you.

How I desire.

How I marvel at you.

I need, I want, I capture your sweetness.

I, beside you, feel your body envelop me

With all its charms

Making me sing.

Unbelievable love.

Dawn is watching us.

Pierce me with your beauty.

Release your soaring passion,

Your lustful breath.

Oh, deep inside me.

The pleasure of you.

Mary CH

The quest

Answering emails on the dating site,
Hoping you'll like me, will I like you?
If I try hard enough, I might…

"My ideal woman wouldn't nag and fight!"
Trust me, I like a peaceful living too!
Answering emails on the dating site.

Can I convey my smile is bright,
The interesting activities I do?
If I try hard enough, I might…

"She mustn't go for nagging, gossip, spite!"
Take it from me, I've charm enough for two…
Answering emails on the dating site.

Some people's attitudes give me a fright!
Can I stay safe and work out who is who?
If I try hard enough, I might…

Some day perhaps I'll find my Mister Right,
In all those members there must be a few.
Answering emails on the dating site,
If I try hard enough, I might…

Carol Wilson

Grandma in Connecticut

When I am Grandma, I sleep in the top bunk bed, my husband sleeps below me. I climb down the little ladder at the end of my bed, shaking the whole bed, drawing it to me with my weight, and tiptoe out to the toilet. The flames from the woodstove send shadows up the wall and cast flickering light on the bedroom door, open to where the boys sleep on bunk beds too.

There's banging on our bedroom door at 6:30 am and a two-and-a-half-year-old shouts, "Anyone want to buy a digger?" Then three children appear with a stack of books and climb up the ladder and the day has begun.

I quietly take my yoga mat out of the closet and unroll it on the floor. A quick stretch before breakfast. Oh, here comes the purple yoga mat and now it's perpendicular to mine and now I'm sharing my yoga mat too – with a hulahoop and two children in pyjamas – and I'm being asked to be the PE teacher.

I sit on a child's chair with my cereal and I butter toast, pour more apple juice and am ready to rescue the baby in her chair on the floor from prodding fingers and elbows and heavy-duty hugs from her sister.

When I am Grandma – and this is the best part – I get to walk around Fuller Mountain Pond with my six-year-old grandson who has filled his backpack with a bottle of water, a compass, three pencils, a muffin to share and three Graham Crackers. He finds himself a walking stick and we head off around the pond. I record our findings in the same little black notebook we've used here before. We wonder if we'll see the water snakes today. I love this quiet place, so still and yet throbbing with life. We record salamanders, dragonflies, and little minnows but really we are headed for the bridge.

He's asked to go there today with just me and I feel privileged.

Last week at the spill-way, we counted three snakes and witnessed the drama of one of them trying to swallow a bullfrog. I said it was nature and we mustn't interfere. After a long struggle, the frog escaped by pushing against the snake with his hind legs. Now we stand still and scrutinize the banks. And then we spot them – it has to be more than two snakes all piled on the far bank. We sit down. Liam turns his baseball cap around backwards and gets out the muffin. We wait and watch. There's a restrained expectancy in the mid-day quiet. Sometimes the pile of snakes twitches. I suggest, in a whisper, that we go to the opposite bank to take a close-up picture. One snake hurtles itself into the water and disappears along the bank. We count four heads in among the coiled bodies. We are patient but nothing changes. Silently, we leave, walking along the path, now in search of the broken-down beaver pond.

When I am Grandma, I love these moments of being trusted. I love sharing my enthusiasm and the joy of it being received, absorbed and returned by an equally enthusiastic kindred spirit. I like being needed for who I am, for the little bit of knowledge I have that can go such a long way.

Most of all, I love the thrill of seeing young life emerge – radiant and curious and eager to be a part of our miraculous world.

Berta Money

Cherish the ladies

November. Rainy days.
The summer was sunny long.
Soon, needles of old gold will be gone.
Shoulder by shoulder, pagodas of larch
hint at Japan on a Leitrim hillside.
Last night I watched the moon
on her back, being tickled by stars.
This morning I woke with no plan.
How to live a passionate life at fifty-three?
This is not a song, or a prayer.
Cherish the Ladies the name of a tune.
How will I cherish me?

How will I cherish me?
Cherish the Ladies the name of a tune.
This is not a song or a prayer.
How to live a passionate life at fifty-three?
This morning I woke with no plan.
On her back, being tickled by stars,
last night I watched the moon
hint at Japan on a Leitrim hillside:
shoulder by shoulder, pagodas of larch.
Soon needles of old gold will be gone.
The summer was sunny long.
November. Rainy days.

Eibhlín Nic Eochaidh

Goddess of Knocknashee

Carly Hillier

A Remembering slice of mid-life

"I count myself in nothing else so happy,
As in a soul remembering my good friends."

William Shakespeare
Richard II. Act 2, Scene 3; 46-7

Travelling these last pages, our companions are nostalgia and bittersweet memories. There are glimpses of significant people and events in these women's first half-slices, suggestions of times past, words spoken, associations deeply made. Panoramas of places known in earlier life come into focus, many with a local view. In their remembering, these women have opened up. They have shared tears and heartaches with much honesty and depth of feeling. Some slices of remembering feel raw and exposed, and even shocking, while others are softer, more philosophical. There is honouring and celebration, and looking forward without losing touch with what has gone before.

We began our Mid-Life Slices with a gathering of friends in a house in Sligo. So this is where we choose to end, among the hills and lakes, the beaches and bog lands, the streets and the doorways and beside the homely hearth. We may find a mid-life sort of place where somehow, through sharing voices, and being heartened and supported, we all can come home.

Mary

A 1960s Sunday

Sundays as a child were always the same. Preparation started on a Saturday night. There was t
weekly bath, all of us scrubbed, hair washed and good clothes laid out. Us girls and Mum were
done up in curlers, the grips sticking into our heads and our foreheads tightened by the ruthles
applied curlers. Dad would spread old newspapers on the kitchen table and line up our shoes f
a vigorous polishing. All the shoeshine accoutrements were kept in a very old round wicker bas
with broken edges. Tins of shoe polish, brushes of all sizes, shoe laces, shoe trees, a shoehorn
and at the bottom dozens of dusty old cloths for the final polish. He kept the dog's metal comb
there and poor Beau the Pomeranian would endure a vigorous brushing amid yelps in front of t
study fire. While Dad polished, Mum steeped the marrowfats and made the Chivers jelly. She
looked severe in her curlers and I was glad she only wore them once a week.

Sunday mornings were always a rush. Mum would bring a large pot of tea and toast with
marmalade to her and Dad's bedroom. We would crowd onto the end of the bed and munch toas
Mum hurried and scolded us through getting dressed, finding hats or mantillas, prayer books an
money for the collection. In church, we sat in the front seats reserved for us (Dad was Senior
Psychiatrist at Castlebar Hospital), trapped between our parents, with no distracting heads in fro
of us. If the sermon lasted longer than seven minutes, Dad would take out his hankie and blow
nose very loudly. He believed that the attention span of his patients demanded a short sermon.

After Mass, we raced back home, scattering cats and spooking the colony of crows that
rose in a black cloud into the sky. Mum would serve up a big fry: rashers, sausages, black and
white pudding, bright yellow fried eggs and slice after slice of white soda bread, all washed dow
with tea from the big brown enamel teapot. One victim would be collared to help wash up and t
rest of us escaped to play in the wood or read our library books while sprawled across our beds.

We diligently worked up an appetite for the obligatory Sunday roast. Mum baked while e oven was on, too thrifty to waste the electricity. Tarts and swiss rolls jostled with the roast ef and Yorkshire puds. Vegetables and potatoes simmered on the range. We ate enormous tes of meat, vegetables and glossy gravy.

The afternoon drive was again obligatory. We all piled into the old Ford Consul, girls in e back and baby brother sharing the bench front seat with the parents. No seat belts in those s. We would race onto the beach at Bertra, warned by Mum – no swimming for an hour after ner. Dad would prop the transistor on the bonnet of the car, light a cigarette and listen to the tch. Mum would station herself near to us, one eye on her knitting and one on us in the water. er our swim we would retreat to the heat of the car and then, on the way home, we stopped for cream cones in Westport.

Tea would be a salad of ham and lettuce with tomatoes followed by apple tart or queen es. I do not understand how we could eat so much, but then we never sat still. The Rosary called by Mum as we all knelt in the study, our elbows resting on the armchair seats, and d would tease the dog to annoy Mum. She would finish the Decades, go through the trimmings d then announce with satisfaction, "That didn't take long!"

At eight o'clock, I would start getting butterflies in my stomach at the thought of Monday ning and school. I would retreat to the kitchen table and make a stab at homework. Dad ght appear and, with the help of a cigarette, get me through a page of fractions and an Irish m. We would watch the telly all squashed up on the couch, and at ten o'clock we had cream ckers, butter, jam and tea. Then upstairs to bed to dream of summer holidays and swims on tra beach.

la Gilvarry

Sunday Reading

My hand burrowed sideways out from underneath the bedclothes that were snuggled up to my ears. With an outstretched arm and extended index finger, I automatically switched on the radio that was strategically placed at the bedside. The eight o'clock news headlines were being read. I drifted back to sleep as the same mantra about finance, European banks, world banks, default and burning bonds was being repeated once again. I was brought to full consciousness with the headline that, on Sunday next, July 10th, the final edition of 'The News of the World' was being published.

I immediately thought of my father who bought 'The News of the World' every Sunday and read it from cover to cover. My mother wasn't happy with such a paper being brought into the house, saying it was a bad influence on the children. She got rid of it as soon as my father was finished reading it, but not before my siblings and myself had sneaked a quick read of it. Then, as now, the articles in it were the latest sex and corruption scandals involving high profile personalities and government ministers. We knew about Christine Keeler and the Profumo Affair, Marilyn Monroe's death by a drug overdose, the great train robbery, the Moors Murders, the notorious Kray twins and many more sensational stories.

Like a neon light, memories of my first year in secondary school flashed before me. About a month into the school year, the Christian Doctrine teacher came into the classroom carrying a bundle of newspapers. After placing them on her desk, and saying the prayer before class began, she proceeded to ask each pupil to name which papers their parents read on Sunday. I was hearing the names of papers I had never heard before: 'The Angelus', 'The Irish Catholic', 'The Catholic Standard' and others. At last she asked me what papers were read in my home. In my innocence I said, "The Sunday Press and The News of the World."

She reacted as if she had been hit with a bolt of lightning. Her face reddened, her body ook and, when she eventually found her voice, it was high pitched and shrill. Then calming wn some, she asked me in which shop the papers were bought. However, I caused another htning strike when I said they were bought from the paper van outside the chapel. All the girls the class were staring at me, except one – she was looking straight ahead and was very rvous. I knew immediately that it was her father who was the owner of the van. To her relief, I sn't asked who the seller was.

At the end of the school day, I was given a letter dressed to my parents. When my mother read it, I saw the k of shock on her face and she became very flustered. thout saying anything, she folded it, put it in her apron :ket and continued with her chores. That night when we re all in bed, I could hear a heated discussion coming from parent's room. I instinctively knew it was the contents of letter being discussed. Before going to school the next rning, my father took me aside and said that, if I was asked in what papers he brought into the house, I was to say he d stopped buying 'The News of the World'. He continued to / it every Sunday until his death.

Sunday 10th July 2011, I bought a copy of the final edition The News of the World' in memory of my father.

Philip McCaffrey

e McCaffrey

File and save

Like my grandmother now ... by Cheryl Savageau

I save myself by not letting go
of all things old and out of date –
postcards from people I no longer know
newspapers, wrapping paper
rags for a patchwork quilt.

I save buttons in jars and in biscuit tins –
lost ones found on floors and chairs
old ones gathered on a piece of string.
I save corks out of wine bottles,
bits of wool, silk scarves, flat stones
that ribbon the shore where geese rise
like a blanket in wind.

I save your voice, your laugh, the smell
of your skin, my mother's reading glasses
my father's last breath, the sound of love
the words - all tied up in a bundle
at the back of some drawer.

Olivia Kenny McCarthy

Nature's loving ways

The snow has fallen
covering the garden, the cars, the roof tops
with a white carpet of snow.
As we glide and slide down the garden path
I throw a snowball at you.

The daffodils blooming, swaying, dancing in the breeze.
Our garden is covered in a sea of yellow.
You bend, pick one and give it to me.

The sun is shining, summer is here.
We lie in our deck chairs.
You hand me a soda and I say "Thank you, dear."

The brown leaves have fallen,
Their time is done. Autumn is here.
You sweep away the dead leaves in our pathway
in case I might fall.

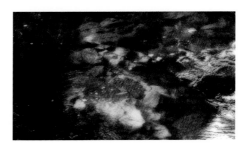

Whatever the weather, it always reminds me of you.

Joan O'Connell

Other Julys

In memory of Bridget

Four hard years accepted stoically,
And now on a sun soaked Saturday
In mid July under glorious heat
From a clear blue sky, it is accomplished.

A long life of love and labour ended
Finally, forever freed from the daily ritual
Of dependency without
Any hope except a final release.

Memories of warm welcoming laughter
Wrinkling your sunny face with toothless smiles.
Your strong dark hair, abundant and curly
A halo about your head, promise of hope.

Standing at an open door, your hand
Raised in sad goodbye, we watch your face
And we feel your love reach out to us
Following us home, sustaining us.

Starlings burst upwards into a clear blue sky
A startling chorus of wings working wildly.
You cannot see them now but once you did
Lifting your gaze, marvelling at their flight.

I see you striding towards the seashore
Your skirt held up about your knees, your arms
Swinging strongly as you greet the waves
Blessing yourself with the frothy foam.

You reached out to life and pulled it close
Grabbed happiness when and where you could
You welcomed the pain of life amid the joys
You had other Julys and we are consoled.

Eileen Sheridan

Small blessing

In memory of Mary Houlihan, née Byrnes

Adrift from the moorings of her mind
she once stood in the doorway of your bedroom
and said: "Who's that strange man in your bed?"
The strange man was your husband.
Life had fallen back to a time when you were a girl
before men and beds.

On her way to communion on Sunday
in her blue-and-cream turban,
her fox-fur stole, her flecked-tweed coat,
there was no sign to show she was lost
at sea with no landmarks, no lighthouse
no compass, no stars.

Sometimes

she knew enough of who she was

to know who she was not

how far she had drifted

from the sharp mind of the mathematics teacher

the mother of five, the mistress of the house

the one-time lover of a long dead husband

the keeper of a garden with apple trees.

Small islands of knowing,

frantic to not disappear again in the mist

that she knew, in each terrifying moment

of anxious lucidity, was her usual state.

But always the mist reclaimed her.

Her islands of mind

grew smaller.

Monica Corish

Killanin

On a July night we took a shortcut,
a graveyard stroll amid plastic flowers.

Jokes about longevity and I asked where you
'being American' would like to be buried?

'Bury me in Killanin. I'll be looking up at you.'

On an October day I followed the hearse,
real flowers, no jokes.

I laid you to rest alone in a double plot.

They say one should not talk about it
but now I am glad we had that talk

although I never felt you looking up at me.

Jean Folan

As her past fades away   Carmel McNamee

For Catherine

In memory of my special friend, Catherine Devaney
who accompanied me through the ups-and-downs of mid-life.
Her leaving has made me appreciate mid-life even more.

At first the words won't come,
dried up
in a parched well of grief
where only tears give life to arid thoughts.

But thoughts are all I have to make sense
of futile fate
and jumbled memories
that lurk round every corner
refusing to be ignored.

I see you on the stage,
your perfect timing
understated,
I see you in the Bistro
where we bantered and debated
over pizza and red wine.

But mostly
I see you at work
sitting at your desk,
I see you lift your head
and feel the warmth of your smile
as I open the door,
I hear the familiar tone of your voice
and sense the calming comfort
of our intimate chatter
about nothing more than nothing.

Two friends
Two coffees
Two minutes stolen from a hectic day
Too short

Because now I have to find
the words to say
   "Goodbye"
to the friend I loved.

Maureen Howley

In Darby's Drapery on Harmony Hill
old ghosts rattled their chains.
Echoes of a tune you hummed whilst
wrapping my mohair scarf
in a butcher's parcel.
It made your day more lilac than blue on Harmony Hill.

On Harmony Hill more lilac than blue,
my head full of echoes,
ghosts rattled their chains,
on Harmony Hill, on Harmony Hill.

The cross, broken from a chain
of rosary beads you pushed into my hand,
cheap and tacky has lain in
my purse for years,
tackier now from blue green coins.
Like my scarf, more lilac than blue on Harmony Hill.

On Harmony Hill more lilac than blue,
my head full of echoes,
ghosts rattled their chains,
on Harmony Hill, on Harmony Hill.

As I tether now at frayed edges
echoes of ancestors in queues unravel in me,
implore me to listen
to the music and
weave the threads of my own life.

On Harmony Hill more lilac than blue,
my head full of echoes,
ghosts rattled their chains,
on Harmony Hill, on Harmony Hill.

Rosaleen Glennon

"I lived outside Ireland for many years and longed to return home.
This was written after a summer trip to Sligo."

Unexpected therapy

Not all transactions are financial. Sometimes no money changes hands at all. Today, it sounds shocking that a healthy young woman might willingly hand over a newborn infant to complete strangers.

Indeed, it is not as common as it used to be. It has become one of those 'visions of the past' that we can conjure up when we need to claim that we are becoming more civilized over time.

I hope we are.

In 1972, I handed my newborn baby over to the nurses. I believed I was doing the best for her. She would have two parents who would love her and provide for her in a way that I could not.

My family, my doctor and the social worker had explained this to me over and over again. And yet, there was some deep, hidden part of me that did not agree. I had second thoughts right up until the last minute. When she was gone, a dark cloud settled over me and I felt myself descend into the earth.

The earth drew me into her warm embrace. I longed to make my way within, lose myself in the eternal womb.

I resented the air that forced itself into my lungs in rhythmic succession.

I resisted the water that sought to rinse the earth away from me.

I shunned the fire with its proffered warmth and comfort.

My family, my doctor and the social worker muttered in the air above my head. I paid no heed. I was trying to take nothing from the air. The word 'psychiatrist' breached my defences and later, in a new voice, the word 'grief' and then 'electric shock therapy'.

I was moved into a bright airy room. I felt cold and exposed. They made me wash. I felt the water strip away the earth, my comfort, as they had already stripped me of my child. I did not speak. I did not fight. I simply pictured the warm dark of the earth and closed my eyes.

Then came the fire, an arching blue bolt shot through the darkness around me. Other colours followed: red, orange, yellow, green. They formed into blocks and moved about, a kaleidoscope of stained glass.

I saw myself, an afterglow as the hues resolved. The browns and greens of earth clustered protectively about my belly. The reds, yellows and oranges, still warm from the fire, settled on my chest. The deep blues of water washed over me from head to toe, without dousing the fire, and settled at my feet. The clear white lights and pale blues of air settled about my head and began to fill my lungs, fanning rather than extinguishing the fire in my chest.

I began to breathe deeply. To embrace life-giving air again. I scooped the earth tones from about my belly and began to feed the fire with them. Each piece felt like another goodbye. My tears fell to join the water at my feet. The fire of my anger burned brighter.

When the last piece of earth had been fed to the fire, my grief was gone. I was left with my anger and a strong sense of purpose. My family, my doctor and the social worker were about to get more than they had bargained for.

Pippa Black

A stitch in time

We call ourselves 'Stitch Sisters'. We are a community of women who individually explored the theme of maternal legacy by stitching personal samplers to be passed on to the next generation. The emphasis for the content of the sampler was women's lives, including themes of looking back, love, loss, transition and moving on. The content of my embroidered sampler is very personal and may require some explanation.

The boxing gloves represent my dad and his success at boxing, both in the ring and coaching. The 'hanging-up' of the gloves sadly mirrors his death in 2010. However, the scroll over the gloves highlights 2011 as the centenary year of the Irish Amateur Boxing Association.

The Singer sewing machine is the emblem that reflects my mother's skill at dressmaking which was called upon all through my childhood.

The three cross-stitched carnations signify my siblings and me.

The maps of Egypt and Ireland show the nationality of my husband and myself, followed by a Celtic knot representing our marriage, worked in the colours of our national flags; the sea being an analogy for the exciting but unpredictable journey our lives were about to take.

The symbol of Pharmacy, coupled with the lamp of Florence Nightingale and the shared cross of green and red, depict our work together in the medical field.

This is followed by the initial and birthdate of each of our children, coupled with an item which somewhat reflects their area of work or study. For example the cross-stitching of the Finnish flag marks the emigration of my third son to Finland last summer.

The four gold beads at each corner (one for each child) represent the cornerstones of my life and how they have formed the basis for all I do.

The sampler ends with the optimism of
an interesting and bright future, one
where I may find more time for my
pastimes – painting, stitching and
gardening.

Roma Sarhan

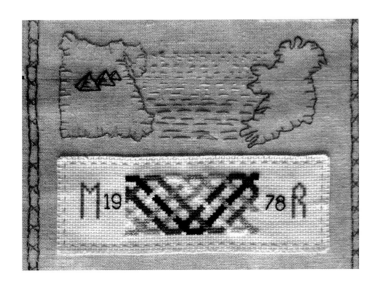

Begging letters

It seems like a dream it was so long ago, but a recent discussion on begging letters dredged up the memory.

When I was seven, I won £10 in a children's crossword in The Sunday Press. I was contacted by the paper for a photograph and, as I had just made my first communion, I duly se off a picture of this angelic little lady. The following Sunday there it was, my picture, full addre and the fact that I had won the princely sum of £10. I know it wasn't the turn of the last cent but £10 seemed a fortune to me even then.

Fame followed. Every relation and friend had read the good news and all were delighte However, there was a downside. I got dozens of begging letters – sad stories, pleas to help 'our lesser brethren' in Africa and Asia. Who sent those letters? Was there someone on 'winner watc in all the papers? Did they have a template of a begging letter on file to dash off whenever the found a name and address? Did they stop to think at all? Did they realise it was a seven-year-o that was the recipient of this £10?

The letters kept coming. I cried about some of them – picked out two that I was going send £5 each: one mother said her daughter was dying and hoped to bring her to Lourdes, the other was for the starving children in Biafra. I used to agonise about those letters that kept coming for about four weeks. Then my parents took the matter in hand and explained to me th many of the letters were bogus, but I was still upset. They found a solution. I really lusted afte musical jewellery box that opened with a girl in a tutu dancing to the music of Swan Lake. Thi cost all of £8. The purchase was made and I was given £2 to light candles in the church and assuage my feelings of guilt.

My friend Claire and I had a field day as we lit up three rows of candles in front of the statue of Our Lady. We were not religious, but really basked in the warm glow that pervaded the Church as we listed out our Intentions. I can't remember what they were, but I'm sure one or two were granted.

Monica Barry

Detail of
'Stitch in time'
by Roma Sarhan

No going back

Objects are like pictures frozen in time, infused with feelings and memories. They are time machines carrying me back over the years, which I would love to revisit with all the knowledge hindsight, all the experience of my mistakes, all the awareness of how fleeting life is. There are especially, the short years of childhood when the baby changes into an exploring toddler in the blink of an eye, when his tottering steps lengthen into a running stride and his hesitant attempt at speech become a torrent of talk. Then the temper-tantrum-filled two-year-old dons his school uniform and my heart swings between relief, at a few hours of freedom, and sorrow at his leaving me behind.

Suddenly he is thundering down the stairs already dressed in football gear, with boot laces undone, demanding an immediate taxi to training. I watch the Under 11s storm out onto the rugby pitch, all energy and desire for victory, and I stand and watch, oblivious to the stinging wind, as he passes the ball with imperfect coordination. I look on as he crashes to the ground and I fight the urge to rush to him and comfort his hurt. When did he stop running to me to kiss him better? Did it happen while I was too busy to see him move from toddler to schoolboy, from soft skinned child to brave little rugby player? When did he start to push me from the centre of his life to the sidelines?

"Bring your gloves," I shout, but he is gone already. When did he first cut his lovely black hair so that now I can see his scalp? Did I mourn his baby curls or barely acknowledge their passing?

Recently I watched a young mother pushing her toddler in a buggy. She was walking rapidly, trying to get fit, I thought. Suddenly I was back there. I was that young woman and my heart lurched in my chest. Oh, for a day back there, a day to fully appreciate that role, that baby, to hug him more, to talk to him more, to kiss him more, to complain less, to be irritated less by his demands.

As I drove on I noticed a young boy, still dressed in football gear, running like the wind down the footpath. Rushing home to tell Dad he had scored the winning goal or at least saved the unstoppable shot. And I was there, amid the hurly burly of childhood with its boredom, its loneliness, its lack of appreciation but oh, its joys, its pleasures, its innocent moments! If only I had realised then how unstoppable is the march of time, how transient is the span of childhood, I would have been different. I would have held on tightly to what I had – each moment in his life.

If I could have just a week again – no – even a day or a few hours, I would right all the wrongs, notice all the hurts, appreciate all the talents. If I had just a few hours to tell that child how much I loved him and what he means to me.

I can hold on to the first tooth, the lock of hair, the first shoe, the childish drawings, the sports medals, the photos of a lifetime, but I cannot get back the time I have spent, the years I have lost, the missed opportunities. But I did what I did. I was the best I could be at that time. I can only be perfect from the security of the present looking backwards.

Eileen Sheridan

Womb   **Pippa Black**

A vision of hope

Today I push myself through time.

I know these things must be memories.

They are not hazy around the edges, but sharp and clear.

I no longer have the energy I once had, but

I don't want to grind to a halt just yet.

I still have a lot to do.

My world is my imagination.

This magical landscape has been my home

For many remarkable years.

I know with the simplicity of life here, and

With faith in God, that love can triumph over suffering.

Each day brings a new horizon and a vision of hope.

And yesterday's joys are tomorrow's memories.

Bridie McDermott

I dont remember

I don't remember
When we met
You were always there
Part of my youth
Teenage friends
Dances in carnival tents
Jiving to showbands
Looking for lifts home
Missing each other for last dance
Mutual friends
Sisters with cars
Neighbours' children
Holiday romances
Novelty for a city girl
Bonfires at night
Sing songs and guitars
Parish hall concerts
Priests and curfews
Neighbours and telltales
Station mass in your house

My first experience
Dancing in the kitchen
Music and the craic
Cows calving
Haymaking
Straw hats
Rolled up sleeves
Freckles and sunburn
Dr. Scholls and fake tan
Then the lost earring
An excuse to meet
In the big city.
Seven years later
Happy ever after
Back to the country!

Deirdre Cox

Pauline Croke

1902 - 1991

Walking in line
Holding hands
Behind the hearse
To the church gate
Hearts broken
Tears flowing
We wave goodbye
To our Mother.
We watched until
The hearse was out of sight
She was gone.
Her 'Will' respected
In solidarity with those
Who had no choice.
Their bodies used
Without consent
As they prepared
To meet their Maker.
God bless and keep her
She was one who stood alone
And did what was right
In conscience.

One year later
The hearse stood alone
Outside closed gates
Of Cork University.
Her flowerless coffin
Looked sad and lonely.
Her work was done.
We laid her to rest
With fresh flowers
From her garden.

Céline O'Flynn

Homecoming

In the middle of what, I ask? Am I in the middle of my life? Not unless I expect to be a centenarian. In the middle of work? It seems nothing really gets finished, always an endless parade of tasks. Even those completed, begin their own life cycle again. In the middle of a conversation, "Excuse me, what were we talking about?" In the middle of a relationship? In the middle of a crisis? Ah yes, here we go, there is always a crisis. What is the crisis of the moment? Self-identity is the one that jumps to mind, but, wait a minute, if you have one, I can probably pull a few others forward for review. In the middle of a field, a town, the road (sounds dangerous), in the middle of dinner when the phone rings. In the middle of a full-blown nervous breakdown, but, but, but... how do I know it is the middle? Might it only be one third of the way or two-thirds? Maybe I am on the home stretch. I am being too literal. But I have to start somewhere to get to the middle.

In fact, I am back at the beginning, in Sligo, where it all started. Here to work on the project of restoring our family home to liveable status. It is a little scary, that after thirty-six years abroad, how easy it is to slip back into life in Sligo. It does not hurt that my surroundings are familiar. My old bedroom, where I spent countless hours staring dreamily out the window, still holds me in thrall. The view to Benbulben, majestic in the distance, draws my eye. I find myself walking from room to empty room, planning changes, yet simultaneously remembering scenes from the past. It is more the colour, smell, emotion and sensation that I recall rather than the people. The people are clearly absent, but their presence remains. This was never a place I longed to escape from, that honour fell to my boarding school. It was always exciting to return this house – at Midterm, Christmas and the glorious, seemingly endless summer holidays.

In the middle of my family, the familiar warmth returns. Thirty-six years of living away, a loving family of my own and yet the pull of home is stronger in these middle years. Children raised and my partner independent leaves space and time for a midlife slice of nostalgia. I am reaching for it with both hands.

Mathona Thomson

Knocknashee from Whitethorn Farm **Carly Hillier**

List of contributors

Poetry

Anonymous

Pippa Black

Ann Bradshaw

Bríd Brady

Catherine Byrne

MB

Mary CH

Helen Coleman

Ita Conroy

Monica Corish

Deirdre Cox

Carmel Cummins

Patricia Curran-Mulligan

Elizabeth Dowd

Angela Feeney

Josephine Feeney

Jean Folan

Breege Fox

Rosaleen Glennon

Rose Holmes

Maureen Howley

Maeve MacDermott

Olivia Kenny McCarthy

Bridie McDermott

Paula Lahiff

Mary Manandhar

Eibhlín Nic Eochaidh

Anne O'Connell

Joan O'Connell

Céline O'Flynn

Susan O'Keefe

Kathy Pearse

Eileen Sheridan

Carol Wilson

List of contributors

Prose

Monica Barry

Pippa Black

Margaret Colvin

Ita Conroy

Deirdre Cox

Elizabeth Dowd

Elizabeth Fox

Paula Gilvarry

Ann Hayes

Maureen Howley

Paula Lahiff

Anne McCaffrey

Mary McEnroy

Mary Manandhar

Berta Money

Órfhlaith Ní Chonaill

Mary Roche

Roma Sarhan

Eileen Sheridan

Mathona Thomson

Moya Wilson

List of contributors

Art

Maria Bagnoli

Laura Bell

Pippa Black

Helen Coleman

Patricia Curran-Mulligan

Kim Doherty

Carly Hillier

Tessa Marsden

Carmel McNamee

Sue McNamee

Órfhlaith Ní Chonaill

Roma Sarhan

Photography

Laura Bell

Carly Hillier

Mary Kearns

Val Robus

Peter Wilcock

144